D0477462

THE BRITISH MUSEUM **Pocket Dictionary**

ANCIENT EGYPTIAN
MUMMIES

Nigel Strudwick

THE BRITISH MUSEUM PRESS

Published in 2004 by
The British Museum Press
A division of The British Museum
Company Ltd
46 Bloomsbury Street,
London, WC1B 3QQ

ISBN 0 7141 3105 9

Nigel Strudwick has asserted his right to be
identified as the author of this work

A catalogue record for this title is available
from the British Library.

Designed and typeset by
HERRING BONE DESIGN
Printed in Singapore

ILLUSTRATIONS
All photographs taken by the British Museum
Photography and Imaging Dept, © the Trustees
of the British Museum, unless otherwise
indicated. The author and publishers would like
to thank Sandra Marshall and Jim Rossiter for
photography.

p. 11 below: Rijksmuseum van Oudheden,
National Museum of Antiquities, Leiden

p. 31 top: Photographic imagery courtesy of
SGI.

CONTENTS

A–Z INDEX OF MUMMIES

Introduction

This little book is an introduction to some of the best-known ancient Egyptian mummies and coffins in the British Museum. They are arranged in order of date, so that you can see how Egyptian mummification and coffin-making changed over more than 3,000 years. This short introduction will tell you how and why the Egyptians made mummies.

The ancient Egyptians are not the only people in the world to have tried to preserve the appearance of people after death, but they were the most successful. The word 'mummy' (from Persian *mumiya*, meaning 'bitumen') was invented in the Middle Ages to describe preserved Egyptian bodies. The blackened appearance of the first mummies seen by foreigners made them think the mummies were treated with black bitumen.

The body was a place which was home to the spirits of the dead person, and it was very important to the Egyptians to preserve it. The spirits had to be able to recognize the body and find it. Then the person could live on after death.

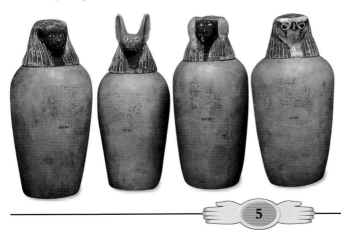

Canopic jars of Neskhonsu. 21st dynasty, c. 1000 BC. The lids on the jars are images of four gods called the Sons of Horus: Imsety (man), Hapy (baboon), Duamutef (jackal), and Qebehsenuef (falcon).

One of these spirits, the *ka*, needed food and drink to survive after death and would eat and drink in the tomb and then return to the real body. So the Egyptians made a lot of effort to preserve and protect the body.

The earliest preserved bodies in Egypt were not mummified, but dried in the sand (like the man from Gebelein, p. 8). When the dead were placed in underground tombs and not in the sand, the Egyptians realised that they must try to preserve the bodies by artificial methods. The earliest attempts at mummification date to about 3500 BC, in the Predynastic period. In the Old Kingdom bodies were dried and lots of plaster was used to make the body appear lifelike (p. 11). Mummies in the Middle Kingdom were dried and lots of bandages were used to fatten up the dried-out body. One mummy from Thebes had more than 835 square metres (998 square yards) of bandages on it.

We know most about making mummies from the New Kingdom and later periods. The more wealth you had, the better type of mummification you could afford. For the most expensive mummies, the brain was removed and the skull was sometimes filled with resin. Some of the internal organs – lungs, liver, intestines, and stomach – were removed and embalmed separately. From the Old Kingdom these were placed in jars and put with the burial. We call these 'canopic jars'. At some periods, the embalmed organs were replaced in the body. The heart was left inside the body.

An artificial toe placed on the right foot of a mummy. We don't know if the person wore it in real life.

Then the body was dried out, probably for about forty days. The drying was probably done by packing lots of natron (a type of salt) around and inside the body. The natron drew the water out of the body (an average human body is 50–65 % water). Drying always makes bodies much less fat, so often the body was stuffed and packed with mud, plaster or linen in order to make it look more normal and lifelike. Then the body was wrapped with bandages, and amulets and other items were often placed in the bandages. A period of seventy days was typical for this expensive form of mummification.

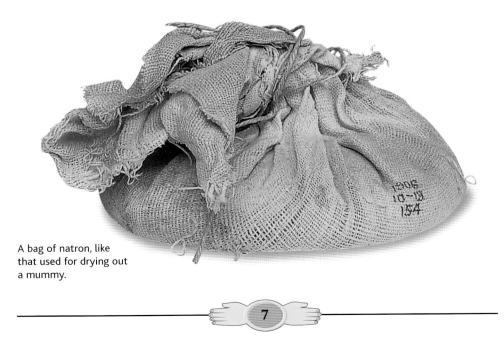

A bag of natron, like that used for drying out a mummy.

A man from Gebelein

This man died about 3400 BC, towards the end of the Predynastic period. At that time the Egyptians were not yet mummifying the dead. He was placed on his side in a crouching position in a shallow pit cut into the sand at a place in southern Egypt called Gebelein. The dry climate and the hot sand caused his body to dry out naturally, so that he looks almost as if he is asleep.

The man's ginger-coloured hair is particularly striking. His face is turned to the west, which even then was believed to the land of the Dead. We think that accidental discoveries of bodies like this might have made the early Egyptians think that preserving the bodies of the dead was necessary for new life, and so the practice of artificial mummification started.

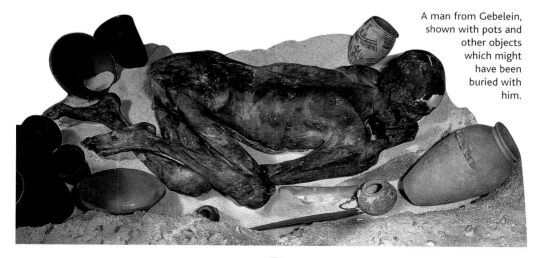

A man from Gebelein, shown with pots and other objects which might have been buried with him.

Coffin and bones from Tarkhan

The earliest burials were made in pits in the sand and bodies were not mummified. Sometimes they were wrapped in a mat or in animal skins, sometimes in a basket. An important development of the First Dynasty (about 3000 BC) was the creation of enclosed containers for bodies, which we call coffins.

This coffin comes from Tarkhan, a village about 60 km (40 miles) south of Cairo. The dead person was placed into a contracted position, and the box was made to fit it. Some of the pieces of wood were possibly earlier used in his house. This body seems to have been wrapped in linen, but was not mummified. Because it was not in contact with the hot sand it did not dry out. Instead the tissues decayed to leave just the bones. Because of this, the Egyptians developed the idea of artificially drying the body before burial.

Old Kingdom sarcophagus

In the Old Kingdom, bodies were buried lying straight, and coffins became larger. Coffins belonging to important people were usually made of stone. A stone coffin is called a sarcophagus. This one is very large and heavy and is made of granite. It was made for a high official of the fourth dynasty (about 2550 BC). The man possibly worked for king Khafre, who built the second pyramid at Giza.

There are no inscriptions on this sarcophagus, but the outside is decorated with a series of panels and a false door. The panels probably represent the outside of a royal palace. The false door was on the west side of the sarcophagus and the head of the dead person would face it. His spirits would go through this door to receive their food offerings. This sarcophagus was taken from Giza in the 1840s and was found in an English garden in the late 1980s!

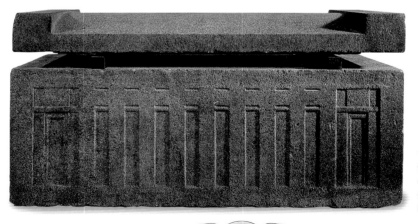

You can see the small 'false doors' at each end of the sarcophagus.

Old Kingdom mummy

A set of model ritual tools for the 'Opening of the Mouth' ceremony. This brought the mummy back to life before it was buried in the tomb.

Not many Old Kingdom mummies have survived in good condition. Some, like this one, look almost life-like. The body was dried artificially, but we do not know how, and the internal organs were removed. The body tissues were not well preserved, but the Egyptians instead made great efforts to preserve the outside appearance of bodies.

They added linen pads under and over the skin to fatten up the body and moulded the features in linen bandages soaked in resin. A lot of effort was concentrated on the face. The eyes and eyebrows were sometimes painted on the outside of the bandages. Some examples were coated with plaster.

The mummy in the photograph was dressed like a priest. He wears a sash of linen across his shoulder and a linen kilt. Priests wearing clothes similar to this are seen in tomb-carvings, carrying out rituals for the dead.

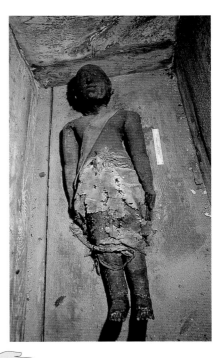

This mummy of a man was found in a wooden box coffin at Saqqara.

Sebekhetepi

Sebekhetepi was buried in a small rock-cut chamber in the cliffs at Beni Hasan in Middle Egypt, in about 2000 BC. At Beni Hasan, the governors of the area were buried in large decorated rock tombs near the tops of the cliffs, and their officials were buried in much smaller tombs down the hill. The burial of Sebekhetepi was at the bottom of a vertical shaft. We do not know what job he did when he was alive.

The burial had not been robbed when it was discovered in 1902-04. The British Museum has most of the objects of Sebekhetepi, although we do not know where his mummy is now. A photograph taken of the discovery shows it as very broken, so perhaps it fell to pieces and was left behind by the excavators.

The outer box coffin of Sebekhetepi.
At the right are a pair of magical eyes.

A model of servants preparing food for Sebekhetepi. Women make bread and beer and a man prepares to cut up an ox for meat.

Sebekhetepi's mummy was placed inside two yellow wooden box coffins with texts and magical eyes on the outside. The hieroglyphic texts are prayers for offerings. The magical eyes are for the mummy to look through and see the rising sun in the east. The hieroglyphs on some coffins actually say this.

On the inside of the coffins are small paintings of objects that Sebekhetepi would need to have with him in the afterlife. These would come into being magically for him because they were painted in his coffins.

On top of his outer coffin were several models. These included figures of servants, two boats and people preparing food for the tomb. These also were intended to come to life by magic and make provisions for him in case real offerings for him stopped. On top of his inner coffin was a pair of sandals. These were not used in life but were there for him to wear in his next life and to tread on his enemies.

Sebekhetepi's sailing boat, with the sail set for a journey up-river. Sebekhetepi sits under a canopy at the rear. The man at the front is checking the depth of the water so that the boat does not go aground.

Ankhef

Ankhef was an official at Asyut, but we do not know what job he did. He lived in the 12th Dynasty, around 1900 BC. X rays of his mummy show that he suffered from arthritis in his spine and left hip, but seems to have been otherwise generally healthy. He was at least 45 years old when he died.

The hieroglyphs on the outside of his wooden box-shaped coffin are a number of prayers for offerings. On one side is a pair of magical eyes. Usually at this date, a mummy would be laid on its side as if it were looking out through these eyes. Once the body of Ankhef was bandaged, a mask was placed over the head and shoulders. This was made of cartonnage (moulded linen stiffened with plaster) and then painted. The yellow colour used on the mask is an inexpensive way of showing that it is supposed to be made of gold.

Ankhef's mummy, with his mask, lying in his coffin.

Gold skin on a dead person means that he has become a divine being, a god. Ankhef is shown with a beard and a small moustache, which is a standard way of representing a man on masks of this date. A headrest was placed in the coffin, and a bow and some arrows on top of it. The headrest was needed to support the head of the mummy in the afterlife, not in the coffin.

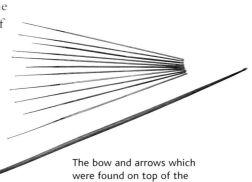

The bow and arrows which were found on top of the coffin of Ankhef.

The weapons may show Ankhef's interest in hunting, and they may also have been put in the tomb so he could continue to enjoy hunting in the afterlife.

Part of the side of Ankhef's coffin, with prayers for offerings and a pair of magical eyes.

Gua

The tomb of Gua was found at Deir el-Bersha. Gua was buried in a pit in front of one of the large tombs of the local governors in about 1850 BC. He was a doctor, and he must have been an important man to be buried so close to his governor.

The British Museum has two coffins, a canopic chest, a servant figure and a headrest from the tomb. The bigger coffin is decorated outside with two magical eyes and prayers for offerings. Inside the coffin are more prayers and small pictures of objects. Gua would need these objects in his journey to the

Inside of the outer coffin of Gua, showing the map of the underworld.

next world. On the bottom of the coffin is a map of the land he had to cross after death. Texts beside the map were a guidebook to help Gua to know what the land was like. The texts also told him what to do when he met the people who lived in this land.

Model figure of a servant from the tomb of Gua, balancing a tray of bread on her head.

Nubkheperre Inyotef

Nubkheperre Inyotef was a king of the southern part of Egypt in the 17th Dynasty, about 1600 BC. He ruled during the Second Intermediate Period, when Egypt was broken up into more than one kingdom. His coffin was found in Thebes in about AD 1827, and the tomb was discovered again in 2001 on the west bank of the Nile. A papyrus mentions an inspection of this tomb in about 1120 BC. The inspection found that tomb robbers were making a tunnel into the tomb.

The coffin is of a type covered with a feather pattern called *rishi* by Egyptologists. It was originally painted blue and covered with gold leaf. The king wears a cloth headdress called a *nemes*. The eyes are inlaid with white and black stone. At the bottom of the coffin are two figures of the goddesses Isis and Nephthys, who mourn the dead king and also protect him. Inside the coffin are the blackened remains of some of the outer mummy wrappings of the king. Some small beetles were found stuck in the resin on the lid. They had perhaps been eating the body of the king (which has not been found).

The coffin of Nubkheperre Inyotef.

Satdjehuty

Very few mummy masks are as beautiful as the mask of Satdjehuty. It comes from Thebes, from the early 18th dynasty, about 1500 BC. The mask was placed over the mummy in its coffin. The wig of this mask is painted blue, in imitation of lapis-lazuli, and the face is made of gold leaf. Gold and lapis represent the flesh of a god, and show that Satdjehuty expected to be like a divine person when she died. Underneath the wig are the beginnings of two columns of texts with offering prayers.

The winged head-dress is usually reserved for royalty, and it shows how important Satdjehuty must have been. Perhaps she was a princess. Her name does not appear on the mask, but it was found on a mass of linen which came with it. She must have been a very small person, perhaps only a child when she died. Her mummy has not survived.

Mask of Satdjehuty.

Merymose

Most New Kingdom coffins are made of wood, but very wealthy people sometimes had sarcophagi of stone. Merymose had three stone sarcophagi, placed one inside the other. He was a very important official, the viceroy (official in charge) of Kush (southern Egypt and northern Sudan). Kush and Nubia were important sources of wealth for the Egyptians. In the New Kingdom they produced much of the gold which Egypt needed. Merymose lived in the reign of Amenhotep III, about 1350 BC.

The sarcophagi were broken into many pieces and the British Museum has lots of fragments from two of them. Some of these fragments put together to make this beautiful sarcophagus, which would have been inside the other two. The wig and beard show that Merymose has become divine like Osiris, god of the dead. The hieroglyphs on the front and the sides are spells spoken by various gods to protect him. Merymose was buried in a tomb in Luxor.

Sarcophagus of Merymose.

Kaitebet

The mummy of Kaitebet was found in the early years of Egyptology. She was probably buried in Thebes about 1300–1280 BC. The British Museum has her outer coffin and her mummy with a mask of cartonnage (linen soaked in plaster and moulded into shape).

The mask shows Kaitebet as a young woman, and her face is covered with gold to show that she has become like a god. In fact, Kaitebet was quite old. The beautiful appearance of the mummy is not equalled by the way her body was mummified. X rays and CAT scans show that the mummy was packed with lots of mud to try and restore the shape of the body. Perhaps even it helped to hold the body together! The outer wrapping is very carefully done.

On the bandages are some ornaments for protection and a small figure. One of the ornaments has a small picture of a jackal – this is a picture of Anubis, a god who looked after the mummification process and protected the deceased in the tomb.

The mummy of Kaitebet.

The other ornament shows a goddess spreading her wings to protect the mummy, and two little figures of a person worshipping a scarab beetle, an image of the sun god. The figure is probably a *shabti*. Shabtis are very common in Egypt. They are figures who were meant to work for the dead person in the afterlife. At the time when Kaitebet died, shabtis were also places, like the mummy, where the *ka* spirit of the dead could live.

Pectoral (chest) ornament with a picture of the jackal god Anubis.

A protective goddess with two figures worshipping a scarab beetle.

Henutmehyt

Henutmehyt was buried in Thebes in the 19th Dynasty, about 1250 BC. She was a 'singer of Amun', a common title in Thebes. She was obviously an important woman and was provided with a rich burial.

She had two wooden coffins covered with gold and a mummy-cover. Among other things there were four canopic jars, forty shabti figures in painted wooden boxes, a papyrus and boxes of food. Her mummy has not been found. We think it might have been destroyed by the robbers who found the tomb.

The outer coffin of Henutmehyt.

The outer coffin provides a splendid image of
Henutmehyt, wearing a huge wig, with gilded
bands and a lotus flower image on top of her
head. What Egyptologists call a lotus is really
a lily, and it is used to show the idea of
rebirth and new life. The sky-goddess Nut
spreads her wings protectively across the
body. Vertical and horizontal bands divide
the remainder of the lid into
compartments which are occupied by
the goddesses Isis and Nephthys and
by figures of the four Sons of
Horus: Imsety, Hapy, Duamutef
and Qebehsenuef. You also
find these four figures on
canopic jars (see pp 5-6),
and they protect the
dead person. These gods
are all protecting
Henutmehyt.

Top of the gilded inner
coffin of Henutmehyt.

Two-piece mummy-
cover of Henutmehyt.

Ramesses VI

New Kingdom kings were buried in huge stone sarcophagi. The sarcophagus of Ramesses VI was broken up at some time in the past, but many big pieces of it are still in his tomb in the Valley of the Kings. The face from the sarcophagus was taken from the tomb in about 1820. It shows the king with the royal headdress and the divine beard of a dead person. A copy of the face was joined to the other pieces in 2003.

Ramesses VI was a king of the 20th dynasty, about 1150 BC. His tomb is beautifully decorated with pictures and texts. It is possible that the tomb was robbed only twenty years after the burial. A document from the reign of Ramesses IX reports the trial of five robbers who took four days to break into the tomb of Ramesses VI. You may have heard of the tomb as it is right above the tomb of Tutankhamun.

Face of the sarcophagus of Ramesses VI.

Child coffin and skeleton

This cartonnage coffin contains the bones of a young child, but it was originally made for an older child. The double feather on the head of the coffin is unusual and makes it resemble a big statue of Ptah-Sokar-Osiris, a god of the dead. The coffin comes from Speos Artemidos and dates to the 22nd dynasty, about 850 BC.

The bones of the child are badly deformed. The excavator thought at first that they belonged to a monkey. The baby suffered from 'brittle bone disease'. The bones are out of shape and very, very fragile. You can see the wide skull and the curved bones of the arms and legs. These fragile bones could break before the baby was born and the actual birth was very dangerous for it. In ancient times it is very likely that a child such as this would die at birth.

Coffin and skeleton of a young child.

The 'Unlucky Mummy'

The object called the 'Unlucky Mummy' is not a mummy at all, but a wooden 'mummy-board', meant to be placed inside a coffin on top of the mummy. The face and the position of the hands with fingers extended show that it was made for the mummy of a woman. Her name is not written among the hieroglyphs on the front.

The British Museum does not have the mummy which belonged with this board. The complicated and colourful decoration is typical of a coffin of the 21st dynasty from Thebes, about 950-900 BC.

Lots of interesting stories have grown up around this mummy board. It came to the British Museum in 1889, and it is said to have brought bad luck on its owners before that. The most famous story is that it was sold to the USA and was on the ship *Titanic* when it sank in 1912. However, the object never travelled on the *Titanic*; it has only left the Museum twice, in 1990 and 2003.

The 'Unlucky Mummy'.

Unwrapped mummy of a woman

This mummy came to the Museum in the coffin of a man. When it was examined, it turned out to be the mummy of a small older woman. Her hair was short and grey, but has turned brown because of the mummification. She died about 700 BC.

The woman's brain was removed through the left nostril. Her internal organs were removed through an embalming incision on her left side, which was not sewn up afterwards. These organs were replaced in her body after mummification and wrapping, each with a wax figure of one of the sons of Horus attached. Her heart was left in place as usual. Her lower abdomen was packed with resin, linen and wood dust.

Unwrapping mummies was very popular in Europe in the 19th century. Special invitations were sent out for people to come and watch. It is now very rare for a mummy to be unwrapped. It is much better to use modern methods such as X rays and CAT scans to learn about mummies without destroying them.

This mummy of a elderly woman is the only unwrapped mummy on display in the British Museum.

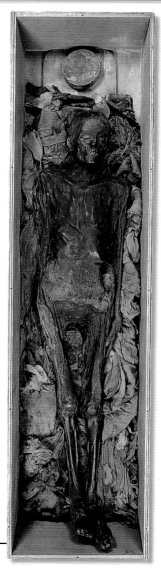

Denytenamun

Denytenamun was a priest of Amun, the chief god of Egypt, in about 900 BC. Amun's cult centre was in Thebes, and this is where we think Denytenamun was buried.

Denytenamun is shown in the shape of a mummy with his fists crossed on his chest. Over his long blue wig is a headdress of feathers. He once had a short beard with a curved end of a type worn by gods and dead people. The two straps which cross on his chest make him look like Osiris, the god of the dead. The rest of the wooden coffin is covered with brightly painted scenes. Below his hands stands Osiris, the god of the dead, protected by his sisters Isis and Nephthys. The other scenes show pictures of the gods who protect Denytenamun.

The mummy of Denytenamun shows that he was middle-aged when he died. Artificial eyes of stone or glass have been placed in his eye-sockets, and his internal organs were embalmed and replaced inside his mummy.

Coffin of the priest of Amun, Denytenamun.

Tjayasetimu

Tjayasetimu was perhaps only twelve years old when she died, in about 850 BC. She was buried in the mummy case of a larger person. This case was originally a little like that of Nesperennub as it was once brightly coloured and decorated with protective gods and goddesses.

Its appearance was then changed by pouring a coat of black resin over it. Black was a common style for coffins in the 22nd dynasty. The wooden right arm is very unusual. It looks as if the original mummy-case had its arms crossed on the chest, and the right elbow was altered after the black resin was poured on it and a separate arm added. Tjayasetimu's face is covered with gold leaf to show that her flesh is like that of the gods, and that she is a divine being after her death. A hieroglyphic prayer for offerings is written on the front of the mummy-case.

Coffin of a girl called
Tjayasetimu.

Nesperennub

Nesperennub, like Denytenamun (see p. 28), worked in a temple. He poured liquid offerings for the god Khonsu, son of the god Amun, in Khonsu's temple inside Karnak about 800 BC. His mummy was inserted into a close-fitting mummy-case made of cartonnage (moulded linen and plaster). This was then placed in a wooden coffin.

We do not know where Nesperennub's tomb is, but lots of priests like him reused older tombs of the New Kingdom in western Thebes for the burials of their families. Nesperennub's mummy case is brightly painted with figures and symbols of gods who would protect his body. There is an Apis bull painted on the underside of the foot-case. Later coffins show this bull carrying the mummy of the dead person on its back.

The mummy case of Nesperennub.

Nesperennub died at the age of about forty. He seems to have suffered from a disease which affected the bone of his skull, and this may have killed him. Some amulets and rings were laid on his mummy, and artificial eyes were placed in his eye sockets. A pair of leather straps, as painted on the coffin of Denytenamun, were placed on his body. There is a pottery dish on his head. This is very strange, and perhaps the embalmers left it there with some sticky resin in it and it hardened before they could remove it!

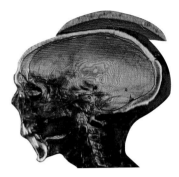

Image of the head of Nesperennub made with 3-D visualisation. It shows the pottery dish on his head.

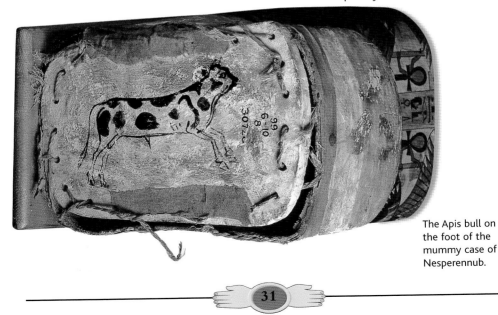

The Apis bull on the foot of the mummy case of Nesperennub.

Pasenhor

Pasenhor died in Egypt between 730 and 680 BC. He is given no job title on his coffin, just the word 'Meshwesh', meaning a Libyan. This probably means that his family originally came from the area to the west of Egypt. Lots of people from that part of the world settled in the Nile Delta after 1200 BC. In about 945 BC some of their tribal chiefs became the kings of the 22nd dynasty, with names like Sheshonq and Osorkon.

Pasenhor's coffin is brightly painted, with a beautiful broad collar and texts from the Book of the Dead. The scene under the collar shows the Judgement of the Dead. Pasenhor's heart is weighed and he is taken by the ibis-headed god Thoth to meet Osiris, the god of the dead. On the cover of his feet he is shown worshipping Osiris. On the interior of the coffin is the sky goddess Nut. Some traces of resin survive from the mummy, but the body itself has not survived.

The brightly-painted coffin of Pasenhor.

Hor

The first coffins in Egypt were in the form of simple boxes. Then coffins changed to look more like the shape of people. In the 25th dynasty coffins in the shape of boxes came back into fashion. They were used for the outermost coffin, and other wooden coffins were put inside them. They had a rounded top, and had a post at each corner. The shape represented the vault of heaven, and pictures of the sun god were usually found on the lid. Inside were one or more human-shaped coffins. So the dead person was going to live in this world of the gods.

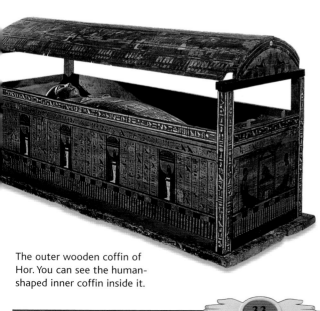

The outer wooden coffin of Hor. You can see the human-shaped inner coffin inside it.

The coffins of the priest Hor probably come from Deir el-Bahari in Thebes. They were made in the 25th Dynasty, about 680 BC. On the sides of the box coffin are mummified figures of demon gatekeepers, holding large knives. There are also spells from the Book of the Dead to help the dead person pass the demons without difficulty. You can also see figures of Isis and Nephthys, and Anubis lying in his shrine.

Takhebkhenem

The mummy of Takhebkhenem has not been unwrapped, but X rays tell us that it is the mummy of a young woman. Lots of packing was used inside the bandages to make the body as plump as when she was alive. Her internal organs were taken out as usual, and placed perhaps in packages between her thighs. The mummy is from Thebes. She died about 650 BC.

On top of her mummy is an elaborate net of beads. These were placed on mummies from about 750 BC onwards. Osiris, the god of the dead, is shown wearing a bead net, and we think that such a net on the mummy helps make it like Osiris. The net is made from turquoise blue tubular beads threaded together. The beads are made of faience, an Egyptian glazed ceramic. On the breast is a winged scarab made of small beads of many colours. It provided magical protection for the body.

The mummy of Takhebkhenem with its bead net.

Ankhnesneferibre

Ankhnesneferibre was a daughter of Psammetichus II, and she lived about 550 BC. This impressive sarcophagus, with its image of Ankhnesneferibre on the lid, was found in a tomb at Deir el–Medina in Thebes. However, Ankhnesneferibre's tomb was built at the temple of Medinet Habu, and the sarcophagus was moved around 40 BC to Deir el–Medina by Amenhotep Pamontu. He added a one–line inscription at the top of the base of the sarcophagus, and was buried in it.

Ankhnesneferibre on the lid wears a tall feather–type headdress with cow's horns and a sun disc. She holds a crook and flail just like a king or the god Osiris. The rest of the sarcophagus is covered with a unique mixture of religious texts. All of them are associated with the birth of Ankhnesneferibre into a new life after death.

The lid of the sarcophagus of Ankhnesneferibre.

Sasobek

Sasobek was a vizier, or prime minister, in about the reign of Psammetichus I. We do not know where the sarcophagus was found, but it came to the British Museum in 1839. His body is not in the sarcophagus.

Stone containers for the body are found from the Old Kingdom onwards. The sarcophagus of Sasobek was made in the 26th dynasty, about 630 BC. It is very finely crafted. His beard is the beard of a god, which identified the dead person as a divine being. Sasobek holds the *djed* pillar of Osiris in his right hand and the knot of Isis in his left. These are amulets which show that he hoped these gods would protect him in the afterlife. Below his hands is a kneeling figure of the goddess Nut with her arms spread protectively across this area of the body. Below the goddess are two columns of hieroglyphs.

The sarcophagus of Sasobek.

Nectanebo II

Nectanebo II was the last king of Egypt whose family came from Egypt. He was the third king of the 30th Dynasty. His reign (360–343 BC) was ended by the second Persian invasion of Egypt. We do not know where he died or where he was buried.

The decoration on the sarcophagus consists of a number of sections of the funerary book known as the *Amduat*, or 'what is in the netherworld'. This text is well known from tombs in the the Valley of the Kings in Thebes.

The sarcophagus was found in a mosque in Alexandria. This mosque had been a church in earlier times. At some time the sarcophagus was used as a water container, or bath – there are twelve holes drilled around the base to let water out. For many years it was said to be the sarcophagus of Alexander the Great. But when the hieroglyphs were deciphered it was realised that this was only a story made up to explain why it was in Alexandria.

One side of the sarcophagus of Nectanebo II, showing scenes from the book of the *Amduat*.

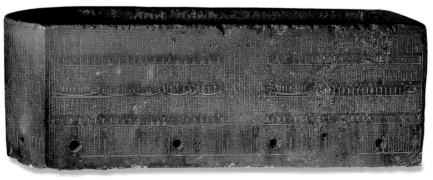

Hornedjitef

Hornedjitef was a priest of Amun who lived during the reign of king Ptolemy III (246-221 BC) or perhaps later. His burial was discovered by local diggers on the west bank of Thebes, probably during the 1820s.

Hornedjitef's burial consisted of a large black-painted outer coffin and an inner coffin with a gilded face and richly decorated collar. Both coffins were made of wood. Inside the coffins was the mummy of Hornedjitef with a cartonnage covering and mask.

Other objects found in the burial were a hypocephalus (a disc of cartonnage placed near the head of the mummy to provide it with fire), a papyrus Book of the Dead, a figure of the god Ptah-Sokar-Osiris, and a canopic chest. The canopic chest is in Leiden, and the rest of the objects are in the British Museum.

Inner coffin of Hornedjitef with a gilded face.

The large black outer coffin has a very wide face, which is not unlike some large stone sarcophagi of the same date. The front is decorated with a large collar and religious texts below it. On his chest is a pectoral showing Hornedjitef worshipping some gods. The black colour makes it hard to see some of the decoration, but black is an important colour as it can be linked to the god of the dead Osiris. The collar and pectoral of the inner coffin are quite similar. The golden face of Hornedjitef on the inner coffin shows that he is like a god in the afterlife. On the back of the lid is a picture of the sky-goddess Nut with images of the signs of the zodiac.

Examination of the mummy showed that Hornedjitef was perhaps about 60 when he died. He suffered a lot from arthritis and must have often had back-ache.

Black outer coffin of Hornedjitef.

Mummy of a young man

CAT scans of this mummy show that it is of a man of about twenty-one to twenty-three years old. The scans did not show any evidence for how he died. The style of the mummy is typical of the early Roman period, with a very elaborate pattern of narrow strips of wrappings over the main bandages on the body.

Instead of a coffin or a mummy case, there is a mask on his head and a breast-plate on his chest made of cartonnage (linen soaked in plaster and moulded). There are pictures of Osiris and other gods who protect the dead person on the bottom of the mask and a picture of the god Anubis embalming the mummy on the breast-plate. The face of the mask is covered with gold leaf to show that the young man has become divine after death, with golden flesh just like the gods.

Mummy of a young man with a cartonnage mask.

Mummy case of an infant

This mummy-case was found at Akhmim in Egypt. The British Museum has several coffins from this site which were made at the end of the Ptolemaic Period or beginning of the Roman Period. They are decorated in an interesting mix of Greek and Egyptian styles. The people who were buried in them were probably important Egyptians whose families ran the Greek administration.

This case shows the dead infant as the god Osiris. He carries the crook and flail of Osiris. The crook and flail are also carried by Egyptian kings – Osiris was in tradition the first king of Egypt. A net of beads on a pink background is painted on the mummy-case. Four figures of the sons of Horus, who protect the dead, are also painted on it. There is a large pectoral on the chest. A series of uraeus cobras are on the forehead of the infant. The hieroglyphs on the front do not tell us the name of the young person in the mummy-case.

Mummy-case of an infant
holding a crook and flail.

Soter

In January 1820 a tomb was found in the Theban necropolis belonging to members of the family of Soter. Lots of coffins and mummies from this tomb are now in European museums. Soter was an important official in Thebes. The people buried in the tomb lived in the first half of the second century AD, in the time of the Roman emperors Trajan, Hadrian and Antoninus Pius. The inscriptions on the coffins are in hieroglyphs and in Greek.

The coffin of Soter is a box with a rounded top, a bit like the earlier coffin of Hor (page 33). Although it was made in Roman times, the decoration of the coffin uses traditional Egyptian images. It includes the judgement of the dead and the presentation of the deceased to Osiris. Inside is a large figure of the sky-goddess Nut, who stretches over the mummy. Twelve women at each side are the hours of day and night. At the sides of Nut's body are the signs of the zodiac, Leo to Capricorn on the left, and Aquarius to Cancer on the right.

The inside of the lid of the coffin of Soter, with a picture of the sky-goddess Nut.

Cleopatra

Cleopatra (not the famous queen of that name) was a member of the family of Soter. This family reused an older tomb for their burials (see opposite page). Cleopatra was a daughter of Soter and his wife Cleopatra Candace. She died at the age of about seventeen years in the second century AD, probably in the reign of the Roman emperor Trajan.

The mummy is very heavy and solid and there are layers of plaster on the body under the bandages. A cloth or shroud was placed over the mummy after it was wrapped. There is a painting of a woman on this shroud wearing her hair and her jewellery in the typical style of the period. Roman victory figures are also on the shroud. This is Cleopatra shown as the goddess Hathor, and she has achieved victory over death and is going into the afterlife. On the breast of the mummy is a small human-headed bird made of cartonnage.

The mummy of Cleopatra with a painting of her on the wrappings.

Artemidorus

The body of Artemidorus is enclosed in a red-painted casing, into which a mummy portrait panel has been inserted. It shows the face of a young man in three-quarter view. His hairstyle is typical of the period of the emperor Trajan, about AD 100–20. A short, mis-spelled Greek inscription across the breast reads: 'Farewell, Artemidorus'.

CAT scans of this mummy indicate that Artemidorus was probably between eighteen and twenty-one years of age when he died. His mummy was found at Hawara in the Fayum area. Two other mummies found at the same time might have been his parents.

On the mummy are a range of Egyptian funerary scenes in gold leaf. The largest shows Anubis attending the mummy, which lies on a lion-shaped bed. Below that, Thoth and Re-Horakhty stand either side of a symbol of Osiris. Below that, Osiris himself is shown on a bed, waking up to new life. On the feet are gilded sandals.

The mummy of Artemidorus with a portrait of him in place of a mask.

Portrait of a woman

Egyptologists call this a 'mummy portrait'. It shows a woman of the elite who dressed like Romans. Her hairstyle dates her to the mid-second century AD, about AD 160–170. She wears a gold wreath of leaves, an unusual purple tunic with gold bands, and a white mantle. Her earrings are emeralds set in gold, with suspended pearls. Her necklace has a large emerald and a red stone (perhaps carnelian) in gold mounts and separated by gold plaques.

Mummy portraits are only found in Egypt in the Roman Period. Most examples come from the area in and around the Fayum, where there was a large Egyptian and Greek community. This one came from the cemetery of er-Rubayat. Such portraits show the person as they looked when alive. They must also have helped to identify the mummy, as these mummies were usually buried in unmarked grave pits with no other goods.

Portrait of a woman from er-Rubayat. This portrait would have been attached to a mummy like the portrait opposite of Artemidorus.

Mummy of a man

Many mummies from the Roman Period have survived. Often they were highly decorated on the exterior. Frequently the quality of the mummification inside the wrappings was poor, and examples of incomplete bodies or even animal parts substituted for human remains are known.

We do not know the name of this man, or where his body was found, but he was mummified with great skill. The features of the face, including eyes and a beard, are painted upon the outermost wrappings, and the top of the head was deliberately left uncovered to show his natural hair. The outer wrappings are very well made and extra decoration of thin strips of bandages were added across the chest and the hips. A very complex pattern of strips was added to his arms below the elbow, and sandals are shown on his feet.

X rays suggest that the brain was removed through the nostrils. The face and nose have been modelled in resin-soaked linen. The upper part of the chest has been packed with a mass of (probably) sand, mud and resin, as has the pelvis.

Mummy of a man from the Roman period, with very careful outside wrappings.

Animal mummies

The ancient Egyptians mummified animals as well as humans. Most of these animals were sacred images of a particular god. So, the cat was sacred to the goddess Bastet and the ibis to the god Thoth. Sometimes even insects were mummified. Cemeteries of animals have been found at many places in Egypt.

These animals were usually kept near the temples of the god and were mummified when they died. People could buy a mummy of an animal and then have it buried in a special animal cemetery to show their devotion to a god. Thousands of mummies of these animals have been found together in some places. This was a big industry in Egypt after about 1000 BC and lasted into the Roman Period. Some animals were very poorly mummified and wrapped, and X rays have shown that certain parts of the body are sometimes missing from the mummies.

Mummy of a bull from Thebes.

Animal mummies

Some animals received very special wrappings. Look at the mummy of the cat shown here, with its complicated pattern of bandages. Probably you got a better mummy for more money.

Some very special animals were thought to be the living god on earth and were given extra special burials when they died. The Apis bulls at Saqqara had their own huge sarcophagi (some weighing 20 tons) and canopic jars. When an Apis bull died there was a special process to find the next Apis. The priests would look at lots of bulls for one which had just the right markings. The mothers of these bulls were also mummified and had their own tombs at Saqqara.

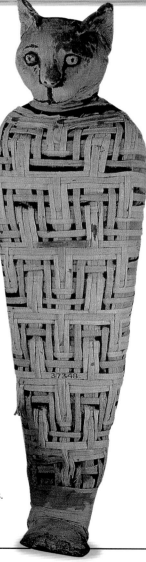

Mummy of a cat from Abydos.